Eduardo & "I"

DATE DUE

NOV 2 5 2009		

2006

Demco, Inc. 38-293

Eduardo & "I"

Peter Johnson
Prose Poems

White Pine Press
Buffalo, New York 14201

Acknowledgments

Alembic: "Trees" and "Just Listen."

Another Chicago Magazine: "Dog People" and "The Half-Full, Half-Empty Episode."

Boulevard: "The City" and "Neighbors."

Bryant Literary Review: "Explanation."

Double Room: "Names" and "Massaging the Ass of a Pregnant Woman."

88: "The Deep Footprints of God"; "O monstrous city"; and "What does it take to be a Viking?"

5 a.m.: "That Permanent Poetic State," "Snails," "The Whole Truth," "I Know You're Probably Sick of Me," and "Attention All Beatrices!"   *Continued on page 53*

White Pine Press
P.O. Box 236
Buffalo, New York 14201

Book design by R. Newell Elkington.
Cover art: *Faces* by Charles Waldman.

 Publication of this book was made possible, in part, by a grant from the National Endowment for the Arts, which believes that a great nation deserves great art, and with public funds from the New York State Council on the Arts, a State Agency.

First Edition.

10-digit ISBN: 1-893996-46-8
13-digit ISBN: 978-1-83996-46-5

Printed and bound in the United States of America.

Library of Congress Control Number: 2005934740

for Kurt, Lucas, and, of course, Genevieve

Table of Contents

Part I

Part II

Part I

This cave—my sadsick head—everyone fixed on a dark day when Death's face shone forth like a show dog's wet nose. For once the eye before the "I." "Try to keep busy," Eduardo says, wanting to cheer me up. "Stalk a beautiful girl, stroke her red hair, praise the curve of her shoulders in a hastily-learned foreign language." "Forget the girl," I say. "Forget the TV, especially." "How 'bout them ghosts," he chants, my head about to explode. And here's Mother Earth with fiery celestial balls bearing down on her; here's the American Sphincter Muscle as loose as a goose. "I'm talking about fear, Eduardo, about doomsday devices which may or may not exist." "Fly, then, false shadows of Hope, I shall chase thee no more." What drama queen said that? Nowadays we'd settle for a second-hand miracle, like last night on the outdoor patio, munching corn chips and guacamole, no fuel-filled planes overhead, no skunks hiding in the bushes. Voluptuaries of all ages, of every species and sex: "Welcome!" And this is how we spend our days . . .

II

Eduardo, wash that finger if you plan to cook tonight . . . I always wanted a friend, even an enemy, named Eduardo. I'd show him off to people, cause a ruckus. Create a chaos like an upswelling of a well—really swirling . . . Before we left the cleaners we got the bad news: skunks had caused a landslide at the dumpster. There I stood, beat-up cat carrier in one hand, trusty nine-iron in the other. This could've been my much-anticipated photo op, but Eduardo had left the camera at home. He stood behind a grimy milk truck, carving out WASH ME with his right index finger. Which might suggest Eduardo is a punk. But Eduardo is my friend, Eduardo is my enemy.

Like a desert beneath a tearless sky, my heart burned. That was yesterday; today I'm all motored out, not even a peep of a palpitation. From my threshold I hear: "You can't get theah from heah." It's Eduardo, dressed like a Yankee lobsterman, come to help me clean my little glass house. I'm sitting on a pail, painfully stretched between two opposite ideas, flicking ashes into an elfish ashtray. I'm pondering the lunatic word for freedom, contemplating an eight-foot-long burial plot, to which a certain Eduardo points. "You can't get theah from heah," he repeats. It's a philosophy of sorts, an aphorism, maybe even a challenge. Eduardo could explain, but he's not talking. In fact, he's disappeared, leaving behind a less-than-seaworthy odor. In his place, a blondie-boy beach bum with a real slow tempo. "You can't get theah from heah," he drawls. Ah, the Infamous Ripple Effect! I'd know it anywhere.

IV

Eduardo likes sex, Eduardo hates sex, Eduardo dreams of a virgin princess kissing the flesh between his meaty toes. Always the same sick dream for Eduardo, so what can one say. His girlfriend's a bore, that's for sure. And when they make love, he says, "It's like rowing." *I can't hear you.* He says, "It's like rowing." Eduardo presses the tip of his chalk to the blackboard. He wants to create an expectation, a moment with no movement. Face this class, face that class. Sure, it's embarrassing, and imagine if they knew the truth—no not that he wears his girlfriend's panties, but that his whole life really is like rowing. Which is how we find diminutive Eddie, adrift in a newspaper boat on his private sea of uncertainty, which, of course, is no sea at all.

Eduardo thinks he's Bukowski. Even wants to be called Buk. He's shaved his head and glued a misshapen rubber ball to his nose, poured flesh-colored warm wax over his face, kneaded it like dough. Then a fake beard, moustache, and a black Dracula fright wig. "Love's a dog from hell," he says, and, "So I walk up to this fag poet and say 'Hey, Little Dick, take a sip of this.'" Eduardo hands me his bottle of tomato juice, mumbles, "That's right, motherfucker." Later, I find him crying over a *Baywatch* episode, the one where Mitch goes temporarily blind. Most of his makeup's melted, little of note except some bagel crumbs around his lips. He knows he should be sulking in a beat-up Ford Falcon outside the girls' Catholic high school, playing with himself as the dismissal bell sounds. He knows he should be helping some whore shoot up in her neck. But for Eduardo, just a little *Baywatch*, a bagel and tomato juice—cream cheese on the side.

VI

What does it take to be a Viking? "Enormous feet," according to Eduardo, and he sure has those. . . . Red leaves rustling or falling like a flurry of matador capes. Eduardo's let loose a bull in the backyard, while three rabid raccoons twitch on a nearby dumpster, shouting, "Olé." I'd kiss its forehead before driving home my sword, kneel with my back to it, beg to be bulldozed. A kind of Sleepytime Death in second gear. *El Doble Sleepytime*, Eduardo calls it, waving his blue beret in the bull's face, then whacking a two-by-four over its head. Even worse, these events never occurred, "all cock-and-bull," as we later joked, searching our neighborhood for the right rooster. In short, friends, in short, enemies, our bull was blind, not even a bull at all, though try to explain that to the three women disguised as cows who led it away in disgrace.

"Life *is* worth living," I tell Eduardo, encouraging him to remove the plastic bag from his head. "Peach trees blossom, water continues to flow." But, for Eduardo, the word "apocalypse" exerts a strong attraction. Eduardo the Entombed thinks he will rise from the dead—a contest that can only end in a tie but without that one special handmaid to anoint his feet. I have come to offer humility, simplicity. Not the omelet, but the eggshell. "Do without doing," I intone, assuming my Repulse the Monkey position, surprised a year later when nothing's gotten done. Just a sharp pain in my left eyeball curling toward the back of my head. How about breakfast and a stroll on the beach. How about reciting the just-now-immediately famous lines: "the ocean stamping its turquoise feet / stranded jellyfish staring at the sun." *But what does it mean?* It means we're anchoring our heart-shaped boats to a nearby piling, awaiting the cry of a sea nymph's flute. Which is much much better than watching Eduardo, the self-proclaimed Fisher King, bathe the backyard elm tree in cheap table wine, then propose to it.

VIII

I judge a theodicy by the slant of its jaw, by how quickly my bowels act up, by the red apple resting on the bleached blonde's head. (Read "question" for "head," "answer" for "apple"). Get it, you naive divinity students of archery, second-rate *hamartíans*, always missing the mark? And here's Eduardo, dressed in spandex American flag bicycle shorts and a delicate red T-shirt. One black skate engraved with a white YES, one white skate with a black NO. He's discovered theodicy in the Roller Derby. The Elvis of Elbow Jabs, the Wizard of Whips. He's one tough cookie. Far from the Eduardo we discovered sitting on the toilet with a plastic bag over his head. So many Eduardos, it's hard to know who's the real one, so just keep moving, trail his sorry ass around a plywood oval track, listen to the roar from his tattooed, multiple-pierced, spike-heeled groupies. No 1970s flashback here, just Eduardo making a point, jammin' with the best of them. "S-A-T-U-R-D-A-Y N-I-G-H-T," the announcer bellows, dropping a blood-red handkerchief onto the track. They're off!

It has come to our attention Eduardo is seeking a mate, whom he insists we call his "wief" or "wijf"—both meaning "a woman of low origins." In short, fancy-pants, suddenly-linguistically adept Eduardo is about to marry the cosmetic girl Bonnie. *And what do they do together?* Massage each other's face and toes, stimulate each other's big hair and lymph nodes. This Eduardo can sure be annoying. One wishes he'd get a job, or be whipped by some leather-clad dominatrix. He certainly deserves it. *And what are his atrocities?* Hiding the AAA batteries to the heated eyelash curler, smashing Bonnie's on-the-go vanity mirror because she smiled at me. Bonnie, please please the insatiable Eduardo. It's not hard—just a little love-handle lipo-suction, or perhaps your infamous face peel. But remember, Eduardo, you'll get no sympathy when the neighborhood pit bull corners you, mistaking your freshly peeled face for raw hamburger.

X

Eduardo has a ringing in his ears; before he knows it, there's an orchestra, the shock of a hundred triangles simultaneously struck. Doctor Doctors blame the inner ear of his inner child, or maybe just a wacky jaw joint. Nothing to do but wire that jaw shut, teach him self-hypnosis. "It's all in your head," they say, which makes Inner Eddie sad. All day he stares at a sky-blue plaster wall, drinking protein shakes through a plastic straw, a suspiciously feminine voice wooing him to sleep. You have to pity him. You have to loathe those Doctor Doctors, or want to tug hard on their pointed beards. Man, they're killing Eddie's inner music. "Bird, prune thy wing! Nightingale, sing!" I whisper, and within a week, he's sashaying naked among the backyard tulips. "Mama Doctors, Papa Doctors, please let this Eddie boogie-woogie, 'cause it's in him, and it's gotsa come out."

Time to fess up: Eduardo has a shadowson, joined at his hip by a number of details. How fruitfully they spend their days: examining a locust's wing under a plastic microscope, buying Santa salt and pepper shakers for Eduardo's New Girl. Today, Eddie and son playing blackjack at the coffee shop with a soiled deck of cards, waiting for the New Girl to arrive and invent them from scratch. Then they're in the middle of the ninth fairway wiping the grass off Eddie's three-wood as their ball nosedives toward a muddy pond. But back to Eduardo's strapping young son, who, in fact, isn't strapping at all, but a sickly creature destined to die in infancy, thus unable to ponder that locust's wing, or grasp the significance of his first name, which shall go unmentioned. A sad, preposterous first name—rarely spoken, unremembered . . .

XII

Speaking of which . . . who hasn't been someone else in another life? Not Eduardo, who always was and always will be. "I yam what I yam," he yokes, while shredding his black birth certificate. Now there's an image with a rough wood-grain feel to it. Today's motif is Death, which I signal by waving my black, faux-bamboo fedora with a white NO! embroidered on the brim. Speaking of which . . . it's not true our minivan fell off the lift, damaging Eduardo's head. He wasn't even in the vicinity. We were in the waiting room, reading old copies of *National Geographic*, Eddie as happy as the wet water buffalo on the front cover, giddy as an air hose infatuated with its own flatulence. Someone had handed him a five-dollar bill, which he gave to me. "You will be blessed if you pass this on," was scribbled in red ink, but there was just the two of us, so I passed it back. "Put the power to work," I said, waiting for the fiver to come my way. So I repeat: let Death be today's motif, our guiding participle, henceforth appearing in italics, like the letters on a gravestone Eddie and I once imagined.

"How to be the next big thing." A slogan on a strip of paper glued to Eduardo's forehead with a glob of hummus. He's been trying to get a big erection, I mean, reaction. "Stephanie Powers Made Me Her Love Slave," he mumbles, shoving a grape-sized pill into his mouth. I'm for something more nuptial, or nubile—both words kissing cousins of *nubere*, "to veil." Yes, to veil but also to enlighten, like the cheap flashlight we shine on the backyard, so we don't trip over the croquet balls. "Pass me a baby carrot," Eduardo says, double dipping into the hummus, then back to the Jerks of Hazard and a certain halter top. It's a bad air-quality day, and there's a click outside driving everyone crazy. I suggest we get jobs, but Eduardo ignores me, grabbing a handful of carrots on his way to the horseshoe pit. Turns out to have been a clanging, not a clicking—a diminutive intruder, throwing one perfect ringer after another. "Why you so-and-so," Eduardo yells, tackling the rascal to the ground, pummeling him with a yellow croquet ball.

XIV

Eduardo is writing a memoir, which is hard to do when you have no memories—a revelation that demands explanation: the real dope from a real dope. A rainy afternoon and I was seriously bored—real lonely, man. And I had run out of booze. You get the picture? Eddie's reading from a tiny notebook he stole from my briefcase: "I was born," he sighs, "near the weed-infested drive-in next to the abandoned shopping mall, my first memory being a blast of lightning, then a great headsin, as impenetrable as an Incan convent." More and more ridiculous images drenched in disappointment and despair, ending with the "red cushion on the family sleigh." "Cut the cheesy drama," I say, perfectly aware of the "red cushion" and of every bird-brain who's ever tweeted in the family tree. This memoir could use a good whipping, a black belt whipping, or just forget the whole thing—don our homemade coconut caps and sip iced tea on our newly painted front porch. Wait to be nighted, then awaken at sunrise to the thunk of a newspaper against our broken screen door.

Be it acknowledged that when Mexican gods are bored, they get tattooed. . . .
Unable to derive satisfaction in the usual ways, we agreed upon something
artificial. Eddie took the lead. The man *does* have courage, and I'd have
never found Rusty Needle without him, nor met the Ivy League girl with a
tomato-sized ladybug tattooed on her ass. We had decided to edit an
anthology of poets with tattoos on their toes. "We can begin with my twin
brother Ralf," Eddie joked, as I bared my massive big toe, nearly making
the Ivy League girl pop out of her pants. "Ouch!" I yelled, but it all ended
up fine: the Ivy Leaguer patting my head, hypnotizing me with her oyster
shell necklace, murmuring, "Huzza, huzza," as the metal made its mark—
Rusty Needle grinning like a hula dancer, everything fine until Eduardo said
to cool it with the bad similes. But I was into it now, sweaty, all revved up
like a hurricane, my Ivy Leaguer aroused, anxious as a winded poodle that
just lost its little red bow.

XVI

O monstrous city, your high crime lights—domesticated stars poised above the squat black nose of a cop car just appearing. Eduardo's on the run, his black collar turned up, top hat tipping. O child of my idle brain, poor pagan in Hyding. I'm talking to you, Eduardo. I shouldn't have bought that chemistry set or sipped its strange concoctions. What horror is the brain's baby talk. Perhaps this hint will help: "I will say but one thing Utterson: 'Blub, Blub, Blub.'" Too many horror movies on womanless nights, too many rum and Cokes, too much buttered popcorn. A dream, nay a nightmare, better off diapered. "Dr. Jerk-Off, I presume," Eduardo laughs, changing channels—then an empty screen, static like the scratch of an artificial leg dragged across a straw rug.

"There's an electricity that's hard to describe," my pony-tailed waiter explains. It's Eduardo with a tattoo of a half moon on his forehead, a huge sapphire pendant around his neck. But I'm barely listening, scanning the dessert menu, taking notes. They're out of cheesecake, carrot cake, mudpie, too, and Eduardo swears he can heal with his hands. "Oh, the night, the night," he croons, "when the wind full of welkin feeds our faces." He's been to The Other Side, slept with a girl whose brother's ex-girlfriend went down on Elvis. Such proximity to the Great One is dizzying. "It's like he's in the room," he says. But not even a chocolate croissant in this place, so I pocket my pen, drape my raincoat over my head, dodge raindrops the size of crickets. Tonight, we'll listen to "Heartbreak Hotel," picture Elvis soiling himself on stage, firing two .45s into the ceiling and television—his favorite book the Physician's Desk Reference, his favorite expression, "Better to be unconscious than miserable." But for now, our socks are wet, our stomachs hurt—only the green lights of the gay coffee shop between us and home. Curiosity leads us on.

XVIII

Entropic Eduardo and I mulling over epitaphs, searching for *le mot juste*. A catchy phrase like "Be happy!" or just the one word "Jingjang"—something to make them laugh. A cloudless day as I jog through the cemetery, gripping Eddie's leash. "Ruff, ruff," he growls, drawing attention from local lovelosters and necrophiliacs. Enough of this game, so we lunch near the dead, extended Edwardian family until a cemetery guard taps us with his wooden club. He's a retired cop with an anxiety disorder. "Can't sit still," he says, and we imagine this mantra engraved on his tombstone in boring Garamond. "Dig the irony, Eduardo?" I say, placing my half-eaten bologna sandwich into a mayonnaise-stained paper bag. "Ruff, ruff," Eddie growls. Which is why I never wish him dead; he's always ready for a good prank, always ready to "play the game"—a phrase we chuck for its obscurity. Dead means dead here. That's the real problem, whereas we like the Valhallic version where we're reborn every evening to share a salty pig with the likes of Odin. But try to explain this to the security guard, who keeps chattering, "Move on, you perverts . . ."

To hang upside down from the top of the Biltmore at 4 a.m. with no possibility of applause. That's what Eduardo wants, then to work his way toward prime time, 5 p.m., when a crowd colonizes and is hungry for a happening. Perhaps remove his black silk blindfold and shout obscenities, drop cat-eyed marbles onto the crowd, spin with arms outstretched in mock crucifixion. "I saw the best minds of my generation destroyed by madness," he'll say, knowing someone's already said that, knowing everything's already been said. But he's not dismayed. He's wearing his lucky underwear, hanging upside down from the top of the Biltmore. A great day ahead of him! A great life!

XX

A lonely life that leads to such imaginings . . . We decide to change the world, but can't agree on a plan. How about a drive to Newport to watch the breakers break, but, no, a calm sea day, so we settle for a cheap omelet. "Mine's a little moist," I say, forking little iceberg chunks of ham from an egg-white ocean. Eddie's wolfing down a plate of onion rings while outside the world's falling apart. "It's a lonely life," he says, "that leads to such imaginings." "I already imagined that," I say, then bicker over bad coffee, the world continuing to collapse, shrinking to this one yellow Formica table. "It's a booth," he says, "not a table." And I know what he means. So let's say (in the spirit of Eduardo) matter really does matter. Let's say I scour our language for a word in the shape of a woman's breast, hold it quietly in my palm, then let it drop absent-mindedly like a melon. Our waitress appears with the check. "We're burning down the houses," she smiles. "We'd like you on for the long haul." Everywhere, the same invitation disguised as truth.

We're starting a band, a real ass-kicking, girl-licking kind of thing. "My axe is the most powerful instrument in the world," Eduardo says, fingering his Les Paul with one hand, snapping the pink bra strap of his fourteen-year-old girlfriend with the other. "God damn," he yells, chug-a-lugging from a bottle of Jack Daniel's. "God damn this wondrous life." God damn, for sure, I think, watching him tongue the girl's nose earring, as she drifts into a drunken prepubescent sleep. Yes, music fans, it's girls, girls, girls, when all I wondered was whether you had to be a jerk to be a rock star. Because we sure is that. "Pass the loco weed," I say to a middle-aged redhead turntabling naked in the middle of the floor, no doubt wondering why her red go-go boots are nailed over the fireplace. Blow on my harmonica, that's what I'll do. Chatter in scat. I got no real words for this Vicodin moment, just a few blue notes mixing with the groans of a multitude of groupies. "Drop dead old man," someone yells from a pile of flesh. It's Eduardo, who's decided to name us The Eduardo Experience—a two-jerk band, noted for its obscurity . . .

XXII

What's a life without animals? Consider Pumpkin, a cute name for a cat, except he wasn't a cat, but a real pumpkin, our pet nonetheless. Eduardo had just returned from Prague where he saw Kafka, who, according to him, "stunk to high heaven." "Well, he's been dead a long time," I countered. "Every child is a book you won't write," were K's exact words, but not to worry because Eduardo doesn't have children. Angry and depressed, we drove to the local Halloween theme park, looking for a pet Eduardo could hug whenever I run off to play with my magnets. I almost lost him among the zombie Eduardo look-alikes, as we trucked through a field of knee-high, sharp-toothed jack-o-lanterns, eventually tripping over a huge pumpkin a small-breasted witch swore was a hundred years old. "Let's call him Pumpkin," Eduardo said, carving himself a happy face with the sharp toe of the witch's shoe. Still, on cool fall evenings, as we toss candy bars into the gaping holes of plastic pumpkins and dodge egg missiles of local punks, we remember Pumpkin sleeping in the kitchen next to his bowl of dry cat food. "Farewell, Pumpkin. Adios, good friend."

XXIII

Ladies and Germs, Eduardo's sick again, recuperating on a black La-Z-Boy, reading about the Island of Atlantis, asking me to bathe his feet in bowls of green tea, to reposition his frozen eye mask. He wants to live in some golden-appled Utopia where every man awakens under the Big Top. Which is Eduardo's real problem: performance anxiety, leading to headaches and swollen big toes. Not to mention he's edgy, waiting for another container of pills to arrive. From my point of view, nothing a good shot of whiskey and a lap dance wouldn't cure. But he likes the attention, and free from sickness, what would he do? "Father," he says, feigning a tremble, "the skin is peeling off my hand." Later, I find him pacing the study, conversing with famous, long-dead apothecaries. "Drink some ginger ale," I suggest, "suck a little Jell-O, too. It's the Blues done got you, Eddie, it's the Blues been talkin' to you."

XXIV

Sometimes I'm cruel to Eduardo, sometimes embrace him gently like a porcupine. So it goes with one's worst self. You could say, "Eduardo's the one things happen to," or "I don't know which one of us has written this page." But that would be someone else's poem, someone else's nightmare. You could say, "God bless Eduardo, he lived like a rat," but, in fact, Eddie lives quite well, with little responsibility: Lots of steaks on the grill and fairways cut short for great backspin; lots of girls if he wants them, and he does, and he doesn't, and he does. Life's loud and unruly when he's around, though not much better when he's not. I'll miss his books of torture, his tiny oval pills, his two fish darting in opposite directions. But we know he has to go—"though remember," he warns, "I shall be with you on your wedding night," then leaps onto an ice-covered raft, disappearing into the frozen darkness of my skull . . .

Part II

Overture

I'm sick of peekaboo metaphors, weary of mad stabs at uncertainty. And there's a guy making fun of my name, a nasty little prick with a Polaroid moment stuck in his head—his mother cheering as another perfect number two vanishes down the drain. So I go next store and order the Stud Muffin sandwich. Try to be friends with my son, talk about responsibility, always responsibility, watch his fingers tighten around a butter knife. And here's a joke laden with loot: We bought a little pug to forget about the TV. We volunteered to open the neighborhood mail, to take deep breaths. It ain't easy training a dog. It ain't easy living with all this cruelty. For example: How many people have I wished dead? None. How many injured? None. How many have made me sad? A great many. I count them while trying to fall asleep. And how's your Reuben? I ask. And how's your Stud Muffin? he asks back, then homeward where we take the pug for a walk, not talking, momentarily distracted by one of those ellipses which make certain historians want to slash their wrists.

The Deep Footprints of God

Are you ready for the smoke? Are you ready for the mirrors? I dreamt that half my ancestors were following railroad tracks into a mine, the other half watching football on TV. "It wasn't a dream, stupid, it was a wake-up call." Who said that? It could have been God. I found His big footprints in the backyard mud yesterday, haloed by Carmine's angel dust. "Existing is plagiarism," someone wrote. Think about that until your head hurts, until darkness surrounds you like the shadow of a giant bat. The rain had stopped and I was outside, pleating a screen, trying to make an accordion for the wind, remembering that dream and how my father crushed walnuts in his bare hand. And there they were—my father's footprints. It was Easter and he had come to visit. He had taken the dog out to pee and was smoking angel dust with Carmine when he stepped into a patch of mud. Yet I still believe in the deep footprints of God, know I'll stumble into them, that He'll part a cloud with a calloused right hand, look down on me and say, "Soldier on, boy, soldier on."

The Half-Full, Half-Empty Episode

A car that's a bass guitar rattles my windows—a ritual I run my life by unless someone knocks on the door. No one ever knocks on the door. Hello from the City where the natives drive little cars with big antennae, where pedestrians lug enormous "I"s on their backs. "As a man thinketh, so he is." But I ain't been thinketh so good lately, indecisive as a blind switchboard operator with two left hands. Hello from the City where it's morning, where the rain-washed speeding traffic can make a snake nervous. "Hallelujah!" I yell, tripping over annotated self-help manuals strewn across the floor—then dead-headed by the sight of two long-stemmed roses peeking over a windowsill, by a saxophone singing in the distance, by the hickory smell of bacon. "The correct answer," my wife explains, "is that the glass contains water." Hello from the City where certainty can be found in a rose, in the burnt portion of a cheese omelet, in the matching yellow headbands of two long-stemmed roses, in a lousy glass of water.

Trees

How many things can you say about a tree? How many times compare it to our crummy lives, stretch the metaphor until its esophagus bursts or bleeds? We cut down our trees. Nothing symbolic about that. The baby raccoons were using them to climb onto the roof and torture me with their pretty faces. "Let me be," I screamed, as they scratched the screen, wanting to lick or maybe even eat me. I couldn't sleep for days, for weeks. I watched the spidery limbs of trees shadowboxing on my bedroom wall, as if something was grieving in them, as if they wanted to be put out of their misery, as if they were saying, "Make it look like an accident." But if by "accident" we mean that which comes without cause or design, there is really no such thing. That's something God would have said, or one of His half-baked philosophers, and they would have been right, for it was indeed my landscaper-cousin who sawed those pretty logs you see drying in the sun, who drove those raccoons away. "Sleep quietly, dry logs," I whisper, before retiring at night, then don my earphones, listening to an overweight actor recite some righteous Wordsworthian iambs.

That Permanent Poetic State

(after Milosz)

As if I were sitting in a restaurant eating a sandwich named for an Omaha grocer. As if these "as if" moments mean anything. Might as well be trying to describe how I write to a gang of chimpanzees. Say "inventory, inventory" and watch them go bananas. I am in good health, whereas before I was tortured by a variety of red meats and cheap condiments, every kind of mustard. I mean to say I was a bad tipper, too busy scribbling in my little red notebook, drawing caricatures of the caricatures on the restaurant's walls. I was waiting for my friend Reuben to show up, so I could say, "Every minute the spectacle of the world astonishes me." Which would have made him laugh and twist his big bow tie. Last night, I dreamt I was the last escapee from Pompei. In the morning my throat felt like ash. "Dreams are terrifying," Reuben agreed, fondling his coffee mug, the waitress frozen like a mannequin. It was one of those *imago mundi* moments, which means "a moment that represents the Cosmos in miniature." It was as if I had entered a "permanent poetic state," which I began to describe to anyone who would listen . . .

Bang!

Yesterday I wondered why the blacks weren't rioting. Even I want to shorten the days of most white people I meet. Funny, how we're not supposed to say things like that—instead, slip into our iron shoes, stumble past each other as if we don't exist until my kid puts a .22 cartridge into the palm of your kid and shouts, "Bang!" Today our smug city streets are coated with ice, a few orphaned birds cling to frozen branches. I trod down to the park, anticipating The Final Showdown, which of course never comes—just a biting February chill, like a February thirty years ago, stoned in the bottom of a railroad car with Jimmy Reed. We were waiting for the crane to arrive and drop its chains. Later, at the Governor's Inn, Buddy Guy was playing. Jimmy said to hang close, cup my hand over my beer, "Don't stare." I was eighteen, two years older than my son, who goes to school with kids of every race and color, yet hangs with his own—mostly blond and blue-eyed boys, tapping their toes to the angry bass of rap, mouthing misogynies while Little League trophies tremble on their dressers.

Hawk

Sometimes I awake with a headline stuck in my head—Doctor in Bangor Treating Elvis for Migraines; Pharmacist Completes History of Drive-In Movie Theater—and I write it all down in my little red notebook. But there are other nights when blood rocks my heart, and people I've injured or the dead appear, hovering above the ceiling fan. The city is asleep, the city is awake, the city is napping. Does it matter? I think, climbing insomnia's creaky stairs to an attic that doesn't exist, trying to remember what is good, what is right. Yesterday, my student fell from a tree and died. That morning I knelt before the dog's crate and kissed her goodbye. I stopped to buy cough drops and a backscratcher. I was cut off twice and beeped at once. My student wrote a story about the Civil War, about heroism. He wrote about an uprising of Christmas reindeer, about a boy and his imaginary camel. He drew a cartoon called the "Devolution of Man," and he once wrote: "Artists have to try, no matter how hard, to love their enemy because it is up to artists to save humanity." Because he believed in what he wrote, he wasn't my best writer. He wasn't a liar; he wasn't waiting for applause. The clap of crows emptying a tree was enough for him, the simple architecture of an egg. He had climbed, I think, to gain a different perspective, like the hawk that mysteriously appeared today. I was walking to class and sensed its dracular presence, then heard a squirrel's lament no more than ten feet away—a bone-crushing sorrow for life, for death.

Attention All Beatrices!

My streetlight, driveway, wind chimes. The smell of home fries next door, a short order cook sweating before a pile of short orders. The paper-thin divorcée: her sadness, her happiness, her blind devotion to her children, her dog. And my dog, too, its belly swollen with kitchen scraps, my son's dirty laundry strewn across his bedroom floor, my wife on her knees, or just the thought of her like that. What's a life without babies? To take care of one's sorry-ass self, start trouble with men, with women. In my life, so many Beatrices, some dead, some living, all angry, unforgiving. I tell them to buy a snorkel, move some place warm, imagine themselves a constellation, or learn to dance like Michael Jackson. "Attention all Beatrices! Isn't it extraordinary being in the world right now?" I can actually say that without laughing, then go back to reading the paper, burping the baby. Even on the coldest winter night I can say that while gripping the wheel of my Grand Marquis as it lugs its ancient carcass up an icy hill. And at my death, when I claim victory, the baby's night light will shine on, my wife smiling in an unknown threshold, the baby no longer a baby, the streetlight the same streetlight, the driveway still there—all my clichés hardened, steadfast . . . No green-eyed Beatrices in sight.

Massaging the Ass of a Pregnant Woman

Hail to the leaf, to the bleeding milk of dandelions, to the boulder under which an ant is eating its enemy! Even to computer carcasses piled high in a red pickup, to raccoons kneeling before a nearby dumpster. "Where to begin?" I ask Quaamina, my Hindu guide, master in the art of pressing flesh. "Personal hygiene counts one-half of one per cent," he reminds me, though it's hard to hear over the wall chatter of our Monet haystacks, over an elastic sobbing in my sock drawer. It seems a pack of extra large condoms feels left out. No! It's an unsheathed Swiss Army knife wreaking havoc on a handkerchief. No! Just a backyard door slamming, then a few grunts from the neighbor's above-ground pool. "From the beginning," I say, "I refused to leave the womb—the bright lights, the doctors promising I'd be a girl." But let's return to the clanking overhead fan, to our extra firm mattress, to the familiar flesh between finger and thumb. "Time to dig in," Quaamina smiles. "Wasn't it she, after all, who invented the sigh?"

Snow

I could tell of a woman I met at a science lab on a high plateau somewhere in the Arctic where it rarely snowed and bent sunlight illuminated a yellow chain-link fence, how after making love, she'd strap on her artificial leg and we'd tape pictures of polar bears to the bedroom wall, share stories of being maimed or chewed on. But all this would be a lie, except that it doesn't snow very much in the Arctic. Today, we're being pounded with it, a few remaining birds wondering if it's their fault, a punishment for something they did in this life, or another. They realize snow can be a metaphor, but right now it's just heavy when mixed with rain, though we laugh while heaving it over our backs, yelling, "Shit" or "Double shit" when we can't lift another load. We know a cup of hot chocolate and a down comforter await us, that we'll sit around the fire eating cookies while the baby laughs and bangs two wooden blocks together as if he's just discovered the meaning of life.

My Life on the Links

I began as a jive-ass caddy reciting Shakespeare to over-compensated bad golfers. I was a ladies' man, too, the best damn door holder at The Club. After closing, I'd ride across the front nine with unbalanced debutantes, watch moonlight pool in the dimples on their backs. Just one of their junk males, but they liked me, they liked me! At the time I was trying to make my life look like an accident. I was hearing voices from the TV, even when it wasn't on. They were saying, "I haven't had so much fun in years. I *really* haven't!" Once I stood on the ninth fairway, hugging a car dealer whose son gave him an ice cube for Father's Day. He was crying, and it made me glad I was poor. "Just call me Sammy," I told him, though that wasn't my real name. I just wanted to play golf and escape those happy voices. I craved the smell of close-cut fairways at 6 a.m., me and the Head Groundskeeper, Red, punishing weeds and dandelions, driving brand-new golf carts over hill and dale. Red wanted to have the fat sucked out of his stomach and go back to law school, but I was content with the grief rich people bear on their backs, with the imported French limestone circling The Club's in-ground pool. So when they wept, I wept too, saying, "Tell it all to Sammy." And on my nightly rides, I'd always yell, "Fore"—predictable, for sure, yet it made them laugh and stamp their pretty little feet.

Names

My mother named me Peter because I was born on the feast of St. Peter's Chair, and thus have always felt sat upon. A few announcements: first, this new baby was not on the syllabus; second, we will not call him Luc or Etienne, neither of which most people can pronounce. He will be named Lucas, after The Rifleman—an allusion unfamiliar to most young poets, especially the one who said, "No one reads Robert Frost anymore." To him I bequeath my three-iron, which I haven't hit straight in twenty-five years. I used to hold my toy rifle like Lucas McCain. I was into coconut then. Now, I'm mostly an apple-and-banana guy, yet still feel sat upon, and no award will ever change that. I once read a book called *The Two Thousand Names of God*, but can He hit a wedge in the rain with backspin? Can He drain a thirty-foot putt with Beelzebub heckling him from a nearby bunker? I hereby report I have a wife, two sons, and a dog. I am not sympathetic to inanimate objects, and nothing will ever change that. For my Confirmation, I tried on the name Mario, but my father forbade me to wear it. Born Louis, he changed his name to John. It took me twenty years to discover that. What more can I tell you? What more do you want?

Dog People

Now that I have a dog, strange women speak to me, young ones, too, with degrees in philosophy and visual arts. One has zero body fat and a nice smile. It's surprising how many people don't work—just walk their dogs, unraveling their plastic bags to pick up poop. Sometimes we nap, sometimes we don't. Sometimes I'll yell, "You with the pit bull, get moving or I'll bust you up." "Oh, darling, my little alley cat," a young girl may whisper, but you know she's just teasing. I'm a family man, by God, and I make that clear. Sure the eyes may go a-roving, but I'd rather die than lose face in the face of my dog. In fact, I'm the funny guy in the park. I once put my cheek to a Chihuahua and howled like a bank teller who'd just gotten laid off; another time, I told a leggy poodle breeder not to be so "doggone dogmatic." We're a smart bunch, not as lower crust as people think. More than just a few hands of baccarat have been played at the park, more than just a few metaphysical problems solved. For one thing, we've decided there's life on Mars. Also, that there's little reason to leave the park. Why become another "folder in life's metal filing cabinet"—that phrase from Derwood who blames his unemployment on the death of his Boston terrier. He just hangs around now, playing with the other dogs, saying, "I'm trying, I'm trying." But no one's listening. The garbage men are up to something grand today, so we stroll to the edge of the park, dragging our dogs behind us.

Neighbors

Street prophet, soothsayer, stargazer extraordinaire. In fact, he's the local loony dressed in a red beret, sky-blue shirt and red pants. Every day the same outfit, pacing the same sidewalk, mumbling to himself or swearing at passersby as if his balls are on fire. One day he screamed at my infant and made him cry. "The next time," I said, "I'll kill you." I told him to imagine a noose swinging from the tree he was leaning on. "I'll lynch you," I yelled. Quite surprisingly, we became good friends. I can't make sense of his mumbling, yet follow him with the baby jogger every Sunday as he eviscerates cans of garbage lining our street. He's collecting doomsday articles, one about strangelets, tiny cosmic missiles that weigh tons and travel at 900,000 miles per hour, yet are only the size of pollen grain. In 1993 one entered the Earth in Antarctica and blasted out 23 seconds later in the Indian Ocean. No wonder he ducks a lot, and why bother changing your clothes when a little ball bearing might tear a tiny hole in your head, exiting your left testicle one nanosecond later. I explain this phenomenon to an old guy walking his nasty black mongrel. A year ago, his dog leapt out of nowhere, snapping at us. "I'm going to kill your dog," I yelled, which made us enemies for a very long time. But now he tags along—three wise men, amusing ourselves as the Earth takes a terrible beating.

The City

Meanwhile back at the branch, the long-awaited return of the cardinal while two saxophones butt heads in a nearby warehouse . . . City, my city! I've spent all day raking leaves from last fall, dodging two yellow jackets that haven't learned how to avoid people. But I have. Even in a neighborhood where prowlers pee in our backyard, or leave behind condoms and Dunkin' Donut bags. Today, I scattered rocks at the base of our fence. At night I opened our bedroom window, waiting to hear a tibia's sweet crack, the "shit, goddamit, shit," from the creep who broke my driver's side window, stealing our Linda Ronstadt CD. Thirty years ago, when he stole *Santana Abraxis*—the same guy, I swear it—I taped razor blades to the base of my 8-track stereo, one night forgetting the genius of the idea, shredding my calf while mounting a woman I would love but not marry. Meanwhile, somewhere in the country—Simplicity: an old man in his bathroom shaking off his penis for the fifth time, his granddaughter asleep on the back porch, watching stars flame up in a minute-by-minute account of the universe. Somewhere moose and little beasties run wild, while people sleep soundly, deliriously happy to be part of Nature's puny plan. But I'm happy, too, gripping the handle of a pellet gun, crouched half asleep beneath my bedroom window, humming the lyrics to Ronstadt's "Blue Bayou."

Snails

I admire the brute dampness of snails. I ate them once in a little restaurant outside Toronto. A medium-sized war was going on, and I was dating a girl I skipped school for. We'd go to the zoo and watch the orangutans regurgitate. We'd toss peanuts to the elephants, or wave to giraffes, hoping for their approval. Sometimes we'd end up in Canada, cubes of hash hidden in the studs of our jeans as my '59 Rambler American lurched across the border. Unlike most stories, this one's true, full of youth and trouble, but mostly confusion, especially about God, whom I began calling "God the Forgetful," saddened that one baby could be born armless, another with two heads. It had become hard to like God, or depend on Him for the simplest chores. Even now wars rage on, babies still exploding from wombs minus arms and legs. You can't even turn on the TV without hearing someone's daughter explain to a wide-eyed audience how she had sex with nine guys and one woman to earn money for a home entertainment center. Makes me want to revert to Plan B. Makes me wonder why I'm back in Toronto, outside a jazz club, eating snails, watching an unmarked aircraft descend upon the city.

Sandals

So hot today I wear my new sandals, thinking about Jesus' teenage years—
was he happy? sad? And why are the steamed tomatoes shelved next to the
raisins? Sounds stupid, but I'd like even a glimpse of Plan A. I needed to
talk to my friend, but he wasn't home, instead off mailing his application to
the writers' colony where he hoped to "jumpstart" his poetry. He thinks
there's another book in him but really just a heart and lungs, and not very
good ones at that. But he keeps busy, waiting for the mail boat to arrive,
chain-smoking, washing down fat burners with hard liquor, happy not to be
trapped in an elevator with his ex-wife, or born a cat and have to accept how
far he's fallen since Egypt. Our cat died two years before I bought my new
sandals, the ones that make me want to bless people and howl Gregorian
chants into their ears, to wear a hair shirt or wander in the desert, even
though there is no desert, just a huge Bread & Circus patrolled by a burly
security guard hired to keep us riff-raff out.

The Great Fire

Since our house was spared in The Great Fire I have been considered a holy man. It didn't matter I almost drowned in a flood or was nearly devoured by a cloud of locusts. I've had my share of diseases, too, and once drove drunk off a cliff in Arizona. But I was spared in The Great Fire, and that made me holy. Yesterday, an old woman on a park bench asked me to cure her. "Of what?" "Of everything." She wore a faded blue print dress and red socks, Christlike sandals. Perhaps she *was* Christ, since He frequently appears in various disguises. She was smoking a little cigar, insisting we had met last year, even though I was living in Arizona. But people have a thing about fire. I once read that "to produce fire in one's own body is a sign that one has transcended the human condition," but I had never swallowed a burning coal, handled a red-hot iron, or walked on fire. If anything, I had deliberately *avoided* The Great Fire, which I started to explain until I saw a puff of white smoke erupt from her nostrils, a hailstone the size of a baseball land at her feet.

The Whole Truth

The truth is I was a fat child, boring as meatloaf. The truth is I was a skinny child with a "very special glow." Take your pick. We make it up as we go along. Not like our baby who spent the last fifteen minutes placing a coaster on top of a cup, trying to make a connection. When I was a fat child I always knew what was behind Door Number One, even when a waitress thought my family was black and refused to seat us. It was 1959 with spiders as big as marbles patrolling our summer cottage. It was 1959, I just a skinny kid with a big appetite who laughed and laughed. What were you? you're probably screaming by now. But you're missing the point. Like when my friend said, "Wherever there are birds there are birdwatchers." Really? Who says you have to see something for it to exist? I remember my divorced-dad drives home, when I cried into the steering wheel and considered driving off the road or directly into another divorced-dad, or when I was so broke I couldn't afford an oil change or a new pair of shoes. Is that truth enough for you? spirit-filled, low-down, and pathetic enough for you? The truth is I live in the ultimate guy pad with a small cache of automatic weapons hidden under a homemade shrine to St. Jude. All day I nap and read the great classics, sometimes watering my plants. I cry at golf events and pray to be the last swallowed headfirst at The Final Showdown. An incredible world, my world! Whatever you can imagine, whatever you can stand.

A Big Tragedy

Yesterday I told a friend my head weighed 8.4 pounds. He was drinking a Diet Coke and touching himself, thinking about the women in Boccaccio. Outside there was a tragedy going on. A big one. Really, a conflagration, like the end of the world, or someone dreaming about it. Whatever, it was very hot. My friend wanted to swap wives but settled for taking turns on my recliner. "I don't like men," I said, "except for my brother-in-law who reminds me of me." Then I told him about our fugitive parakeet who returned home after ten years, wanting to make up, but it was too late. "Do you think my driving is okay?" my friend asked, resting his head on the floor scale. All morning we carved lawn ornaments out of green Styrofoam, then walked down to a deserted corner of the beach where we found a woman's hand sprouting from the sand like an exclamation point. We called the cops and went home, then sat on the porch and watched a neighbor's lawnmower parade back and forth. Back in the house, I said it was the spaces between the ellipses that could kill you. My friend sat quietly, still disturbed by the woman on the beach, by the cruelty of it all. He said his head hurt, so rested it again on the floor scale, where we tried to get a reading, but he just wouldn't keep still.

Explanation

What should I tell you? That it rained for five straight days, that the gutters leaked in spite of the duct tape, that a rat ate through the cellar screen and killed the cat? Today, a bus exploded in Israel killing eighteen people, and no one is paying attention. We pour our oatmeal, cover it with bran, with raisins. We rev up our stainless steel juicers and kiss each other goodbye. "In a brazen daytime ambush yesterday," I read, then feed the dog, take her for a walk. It's been one year since the world was silenced by a ringing in my ears, my jaw tightening at the thought of leaving home. Gone was the trail left by any stupid thought. Gone the long conversations with friends on the phone, or killing time with a raisin bagel in a loud coffee shop with absolutely no fear of being blown into another galaxy, one much saner than ours. But I got used to the ringing, just as I get used to the headlines, to the lies and counter lies, barely audible over the bad music of the nightly news, over Sunday sermons as useless as a clock we once buried inside a snowman's brainless head—its tick, tick, ticking. "As an armor-plated bus lumbered up the winding road to Emanuel," I read. "As a powerful bomb exploded, riddling the vehicle with shrapnel. . . ."

Just Listen

I sit by the window and watch a great mythological bird go down in flames. In fact, it's a kite the neighborhood troublemaker has set on fire. Twenty-one and still living at home, deciding when to cut through a screen and chop us into little pieces. "He wouldn't hurt a fly," his mother would say, as they packed our parts into black antiseptic body bags. I explain this possibility to the garbage men. I'm trying to make friends with them, unable to understand why they leave our empty cans in the middle of the driveway, then laugh as they walk away. One says, "Another name for moving air is wind, and shade is just a very large shadow"—perhaps a nice way to make me feel less eclipsed. It's not working, it's not working. I'm scared for children yet to be abducted, scared for the pregnant woman raped at knife point on the New Jersey Turnpike, scared for what violence does to one's life, how it squats inside the hollow heart like a dead cricket. My son and his friends found a dead cricket, coffined it in a plastic Easter egg and buried it in the backyard. It was a kind of time capsule, they explained—a surprise for some future boy archeologist, someone much happier than us, who will live during a time when trees don't look so depressed, and birds and dogs don't chatter and growl like the chorus in an undiscovered Greek tragedy.

I Know You're Probably Sick of Me

You're probably thinking, "This guy should cheer up." Or you'd like to glare at me and say, "Have a little faith, Bucko, stop complaining." I see your point. I've never heard an elephant moan, "I'm lonely, so lonely," or a seal whine, "It's not fair." On the very last episode of *The Slayer*, Buffy said, "The battle between good and evil isn't about wishes, it's about choices"— words that haunt me as I mail my check for *A Short Course in Miracles*, then take my infant to the zoo. At his age an elephant might as well be a monkey, but he's happy to be somewhere outside himself. According to *A New Catechism*, "a miracle is an event occurring outside of nature," yet I'm happiest when pouring concrete or changing a diaper, when listening to the outdoor zapper fry hundreds of virus-infested mosquitoes. You're probably thinking, "Back off, pal. Take a pill." But how much safer we'd feel if God were a car mechanic or a drunk—anything to suggest He's working and suffering like the rest of us. Granted, not the happiest thoughts for the zoo, and who'd want to piss off God, though I know He'll love me, even be amused, when I stand before Him, saying, "I tried, I tried"—not sure whether I really did.

One Hell of a Year

I've had one hell of a year and wonder when I'll have to pay for it, which is why I still wear my "New Dad" bracelet, which got me free parking and unlimited lousy coffee in the hospital cafeteria. I hold my infant close to my breast. I take him wherever I go. Who's going to whack a guy with a baby, who's going to say, "Give me your wallet, or I'll bust you up?" What kind of God would have man and child run down by a Mack truck, or crushed by a load of steel meant for the new Children's Museum? Even got some poems read this year and won a big award. Got to play with my wife in a hotel we could've never afforded. Got to New York, New York, where the food at the reception was great. And to the poet who said I mispronounced "Laughlin," I suggest a frontal lobotomy with a rusty screwdriver. And to the poet who said, "No one reads John Berryman anymore," I offer cement shoes and a bridge in Minneapolis to leap from. And to the poet who said . . . But, ah, this is a happy poem about the wonderful year I've had, which I know I'll have to pay for because that's how it works: a leaky cell phone, the old bone-in-the-throat gag, caught with my pants down at the Bill Clinton Motor Lodge, dead-headed by a socket wrench at 1 a.m. in the Cumberland Farms parking lot. But, again, let's sing a happy poem for my one hell of a year—for endless nights in damp and twisted sheets, or a simple cup of chai as I sit on my front porch, listening to my teenage son tell the whole damn neighborhood just how much he loves me.

Green Mountains Review: "This cave—my sadsick head"; "Eduardo, wash that finger"; "Like a desert beneath a tearless sky"; "Life *is* worth living"; and "Eduardo has a ringing in his ears."

LUNA: "Bang."

New American Writing: "Time to fess up."

Ploughshares: "Sandals."

Sentence: "Overture," "Hawk," "The Great Fire," "A Big Tragedy," "Eduardo thinks he's Bukowski," "I judge a theodicy," and "Ladies and Germs."

The Potomac: "My Life on the Links."

TriQuarterly: "Speaking of which . . ."; "How to be the next big thing"; "Eduardo is writing a memoir"; "Be it acknowledged"; "A lonely life"; and "Sometimes I'm cruel to Eduardo."

Web Del Sol: "One Hell of a Year" and "Snow."

"Trees," "Bang!," "Hawk," "A Big Tragedy," "The Great Fire," and "Just Listen," reprinted in *The Smile at the Foot of the Ladder: A Prose Poem Anthology* (Obscure Publications, 2004).

I wish to thank Rhode Island State Council on the Arts and The Academy of American Poets for awards which gave me time to write this book. Thanks also to Russell Edson for the title and for convincing me not to kill off Eduardo after the first three poems. My gratitude, too, to Jack Allman, whose encouragement and close reading drastically improved this book. Finally, a belated nod to Bruce Smith, whom I forgot to acknowledge for his copious comments on *Miracles & Mortifications*.

About the Author

Peter Johnson's books of prose poems include *Pretty Happy!* (White Pine Press, 1997), *Love Poems for the Millennium* (Quale Press, 1998), and *Miracles & Mortifications* (White Pine Press, 2001), which received the 2001 James Laughlin Award from The Academy of American Poets. His collection of stories, *I'm a Man,* was published by White Pine Press in 2003, and his short novel, *What Happened,* is forthcoming from Front Street Books in 2006. He was awarded creative writing fellowships from the National Endowment for the Arts in 1999 and from Rhode Island Council on the Arts in 2002, and he is a contributing editor for *The American Poetry Review, Sentence: A Journal of Prose Poetics, Slope,* and *Web del Sol.* Born and raised in Buffalo, New York, he currently teaches at Providence College in Providence Rhode Island, where he resides with his wife and two sons.